RYA F

GW00579995

Compiled by Alan Olive and Harvey Hillary
Foreword by Tim Hall, Director of Sailing WYA

Technical Editor Mike Hart
RYA Coaching Development Officer

© RYA 2009
First Published 2009
The Royal Yachting Association
RYA House, Ensign Way, Hamble
Southampton SO31 4YA
Tel: 0845 345 0400
Fax: 0845 345 0329
Email: publications@rya.org.uk
Web: www.rya.org.uk

A CIP record of this book is available from the British Library

Note: While all reasonable care has been taken in the preparation
of this book, the publisher takes no responsibility for the use of the
methods or products or contracts described in the book.

Telephone 0845 345 0400 for a free copy of our
Publications Catalogue.

Cover Design: Creativebyte
Proof reading and index: Alan Thatcher
Photographs: Peter Bentley and David Cockerill
Illustrations: Philip Twinning
Typeset: Creativebyte
Printed in China through World Print

Totally Chlorine **Sustainable**
Free **Forests**

Contents

Part 1 - Best Practice for Coaching

Part 2 - Specific Training Exercises

Part 3 - General Training

Part 1 - Best Practice for Coaching

5 Steps to Success

1. Introduce the drill on shore
   When using a training drill for the first time, it's important to fully explain the rules, set-up and objectives of the exercise before going afloat. Briefing and discussing the exercise will help avoid any misunderstanding and ensure quick transitions between drills with minimum confusion. Try to involve the group in the briefing, tying in personal experience into the aims and objectives of the exercise so that the relevance can be fully understood.

2. Use a demonstration, either on land or water
   Try to provide a best practice blueprint of a drill whenever possible. In its simplest form this may be a diagram of the exercise on a white board. Whenever possible, try to use previous video footage of the drill being performed well or use shorebased drills to break down a new skill into small components. Kinaesthetic teaching methods are often more effective at passing on a new technique and can enhance the success of on the water training.

3. Running the drill
   Be sympathetic when running drills for the first time as they rarely go to plan. Start with an exercise in its simplest form so that the group has a better chance of performing the exercise successfully. As more sailors get to grips with the rules and manoeuvring required, increase the difficulty and fully explore the educational potential of the drill.

4. On the water feedback
   As a coach, your goal must be to train out bad habits and train in good techniques. Ideally, you will be able to recognise poor practice and to give suggestions on how best to correct the fault on the water. Try not to address too many faults at any one time. Focus on underpinning techniques first, working towards fine-tuning specific skills as sailors becomes more proficient at the drill.

5. Debrief and adaptation
   For most sailors and especially at elite level, the most effective learning occurs out on the water. However, it is during the de-brief that both the coach and the sailors can summarise the day's activities, lessons learnt and any relative differences within the group. Use video footage and sailors' own experiences to reinforce positive experiences which can then be summarised at the end of the session or re-visited at a later date. A final tool is to encourage the sailors to adapt techniques practised for different situations or to tailor a skill to their own personal style.

Using the Manual

Exercises in this book will be presented in the following way:

Drill Title – Standard 'tag names' help enable coaches to be consistent which in turn avoids confusion teaching new groups or working with other coaches.

Colour Coding – Suggested ability level of the group required for an exercise.

■ START
■ INTERMEDIATE
■ ADVANCED

Note: Some exercises will suit multiple skill levels depending on the variations used.

Gear – Specifies the marks and additional coaching resources required by the drill.

Description – Sets out the rules of the exercise and if it is to be competition or skills based.

Aim – Explains the objectives of an exercise, the skills that are to be targeted and how they are relevant on the race course.

Set up – Outlines how to run the exercise, tips on laying the course and additional comments on best practice for coaches.

Variations – Ideas on how best to adapt the drill to suit different abilities and group sizes or to add an element of progression or variety.

Top Tips – Advice to help the drill run smoothly.

Coaching Points – Best practice techniques and coach focused instruction to help get the most out of the exercise. Also provides a guide to providing feedback on the drill.

Effective Coaching Tips

- Kiss – "Keep it short and simple" – Focused sessions with specific training goals are better at helping skill acquisition within a group. Try not to over reach by cramming too much into each session, as this will increase briefing time, confuse sailors or lose focus within the group.

- Session Plans – Outline training goals including variations and progressions. Preparation here will result in a much clearer briefing and that's 50% of the way towards a good session.

- Learning Objectives – Test the sailors at the end of the day to assess whether your session plans have been translated into effective learning, far more useful than simply scoring how good you were at running the session.

- Abstract Training – Try not to fall into the trap of running exercises with unclear or unrelated goals. Sailors always put more effort into rehearsal if they can relate the technique to personal experience or specific scenarios on the race course.

- Time To Learn – When introducing new skills, allow sufficient time for individuals to practise techniques and encourage 'thinking time' between repetitions to assess their own progression.

- Learning Styles – People learn in different ways so be prepared to adapt your delivery style to the individual. Asking questions will not only help to assess progression but will also help the sailors to reinforce their understanding by talking about the skill.

- Progression – Try to include this in your session working towards an element of overload. Pressure is an excellent way of encouraging adaptation both physically and within motor skills.

- Warm up – Introduce skill – rehearse in a controlled environment – test in a racing situation – refine and adapt.

Controlling groups

- Holding Patterns – Control is critical especially in junior, low ability or Skiff classes where groups can separate rapidly. To avoid this always have a set holding exercise and course area that sailors can revert to in the event that you have to rescue a capsized boat or re-lay the course.

- Wind Speed and Temperature – Directly impact the number of successful exercises you will be able to run per-session. Larger or more diverse groups also influence this.

- Good Practice – Encourage sailors to come close to the coach boat at the end of every exercise. This will give you the opportunity of passing on coaching points and to brief them on the next activity. Also keeps the group together and stops you having to charge off after individuals.

- Communication – Wait until boats are alongside or in holding position before passing on instructions. Use a whistle to gain a boat's attention and position yourself to windward to help carry your voice.

- Use First Names – Placing duck tape on buoyancy aids with the sailors' names will help you remember. Engage eye-to-eye contact and use consistent, enthusiastic body language.

Coaching Checklist

Weather and forecast	Time available
Ratios of safety boats to sailors/boats	Facilities available
Types of boat	Insurance (club, personal, safety boat, sailors)
Rescue facilities	Medical conditions of the students/coach/helpers - Medical Form
Sailor's ability, size, gender and age	Communications with shore, sailors, emergency teams - MOB, radio
Other club activities	Hazards associated with sailing at that club/area
Tide and tidal flow	Risk assessment and form

Standard hand signals

Starting

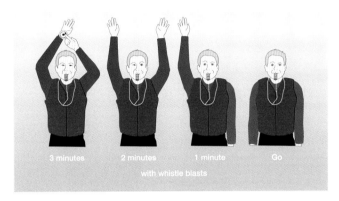

3 minutes   2 minutes   1 minute   Go

with whistle blasts

Communicating Instructions

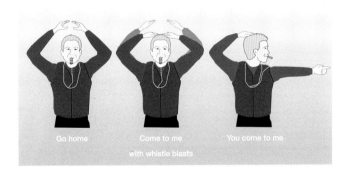

Go home   Come to me   You come to me

with whistle blasts

Setting Courses

1. For fast course laying drop the pin end first and take a true wind reading from that mark.
2. Motor along your bearing for the appropriate distance given wind strength and class of boat. Then drop the windward mark and return to the pin.
3. Take a wind reading at the pin, add 90° and motor along that bearing until have the correct length line. Move 2-3 boat lengths upwind or up tide and drop the anchor. Then correct the line adjusting the anchor line to the back bearing.
4. Lay leeward marks with a back bearing of the windward mark.
5. Wing marks should be an extension of the start line bearing.
6. Use over-length anchor line on starting marks to enable you to change line bias without having to re-lay.

Windward / Leeward Variations

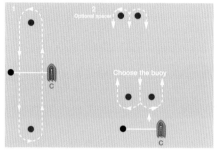

1. This is fast to set up and requires minimal buoyage since all marks are left to port. The start/finish line can also be used and a mid course gate (two marks that the fleet have to sail through on the upwind or downwind legs). This means the course can be easily shortened and gives options for mixed ability groups.
2. This version keeps start and finish lines separate to the gate. Sail the assigned number of laps, rounding either leeward mark before passing through the gate to the finish line on the final lap.
   The final variation inserts a spacer mark to prevent boats hoisting and colliding with boats approaching the windward mark.

Triangle / Sausage and P Course

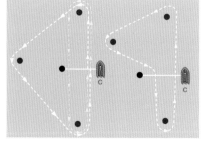

Is the old style Olympic course and is still very useful for training sessions as it includes all points of sailing and a variety of mark rounding situations. The beauty of this course is you can run it as a sausage or a triangle first.
The P course is a variation on the above which incorporates both the triangle and sausage into one lap. By using the outer limit start buoy as the bear away mark at the end of the triangle it gives you many options for sessions.

Trapezoid (Inner and Outer Loop)

Employed by many Olympic classes this course requires the top reach to be set tight so that flying a spinnaker is made difficult. The bottom reach should be a little freer to provide overtaking options. Using alternative inner and outer loops allows different classes to be raced on the same course area, saving the coach time and effort.

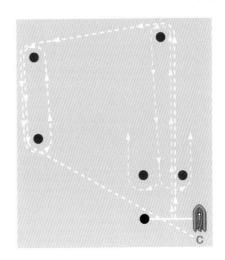

Time Filler Exercises

Can be very effective as a holding exercise to bring groups together when leaving the shore or for sailors to revert to if you have to rescue a capsized boat or re-lay the course.

Reach 2 Reach

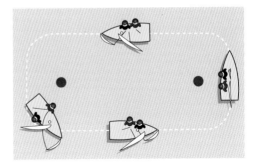

Figure 8

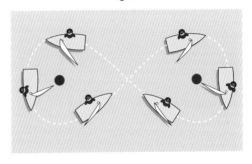

Part 2 - Specific Training Exercises
Boat Handling

Boat handling is the cornerstone of creating racing skills. It can be done off the race course and often without the need of a coach. The aim is to make these skills automatic in training and racing allowing the sailor to focus on tactics and strategy.

Follow My Leader (2+boats)

START INTERMEDIATE

Gear – Coach boat.

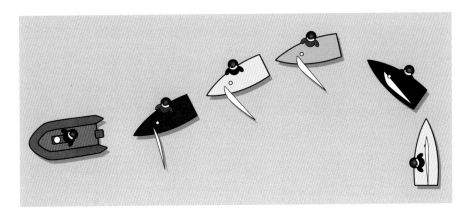

Description – The original boat handling exercise. The fleet lines up behind the coach boat responding to changes in speed and direction while staying as close as possible. No overtaking, no cutting corners and you must react to the boat directly in front rather than those further up the line.

Aim
- The idea is to eliminate the elastic band effect through better boat handling and by responding quickly to changes. Improves acceleration and stopping and also communication between the crew.

Set up – Start with the fleet in a line behind the coach boat on a beam reach 2-3 boat lengths apart. On the whistle start the exercise.

Variations – Mix the moves up as much as possible – stop-starts and different speeds. Try changing the rules to add an element of competition, or alternatively put the focus on control by saying as soon as the boat behind becomes overlapped, they are eliminated.

Coaching Points
- Start Try looking at roles within the boat and communication regarding the boat in front. As sailors improve move the emphasis towards changing settings for speed or control and the 5 Essentials.

Tacking on the Whistle (1+boats)   START INTERMEDIATE

Gear – Coach boat and a whistle.

Description – Begin with the fleet in a line behind the coach boat, on the first whistle harden up onto a close-hauled course to start the exercise. From then on each whistle is the signal to tack.

Aim
- To identify good tacking technique.
- Allows the coach to dictate when boats tack, increasing pressure by taking away preparation time.
- Ideal for filming as it allows the coach to film multiple tacks in a short amount of time.

Set up – Start with the fleet in a line on a beam reach behind the coach boat. Aim to get boats 2 lengths apart, changing speed to bunch or spread out the fleet.

Variations – Vary the timing between whistles to shift the emphasis from boat handling (frequent) to rhythm and technique (infrequent).

Top Tip
Film the exercise from behind and slightly to windward. This will give you an easier radius to follow as the focus boat is tacking. View at least 3 tacks before giving feedback to the sailor.

Coaching Points
- Start 5 Essentials, with so much going on the basics tend to be forgotten.
- Intermediate Look at the rhythm of the tack and highlight gains forward and to windward during the manoeuvre.

Whistles (1+boats)

Gear – Coach boat and a whistle.

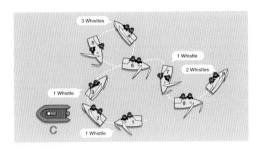

Description – Similar to 'Tacking on the Whistle' but with a bit more variety. On the first whistle harden up onto a close-hauled course to start the exercise, from then on whistle signals denote the following manoeuvres:

- 1 Whistle = Tack or Gybe
- 2 Whistles = Bear away or Harden up (Straight set / Straight drop)
- 3 Whistles = Gybe Set / Gybe Drop or Start / Stop

Aim
- Keeps fleet together and enables the coach to combine different manoeuvres and make direct comparisons within the group.
- Ideal for use as a warm up, intense tacking / gybing practice or for fitness overload.

Set up – Start with the fleet in a line behind the coach boat on a beam reach 2-3 boat lengths apart.

Variations – Try changing the timing between whistles, fast to increase intensity or slow to focus on speed through manoeuvres. Also try a fourth whistle to denote a 360° penalty.

Top Tip
Bearing away and heading up tends to compress the group with tacks and gybes extending the gaps. For a 360° it may be an idea to agree on going for the gybe first to avoid collisions.

Coaching Points
- Intermediate Set the boat trim and balance up before going for the turn. Time spent before the turn will improve the boat's reaction to the rudder and quality of the turn itself.

Magic Roundabout (3+boats)

Gear – 1 mark and coach boat.

Description
Option 1 (see illustration) boats must sail around the coach boat and spreader mark as fast as possible. When the coach blows the whistle the fleet reverses direction.

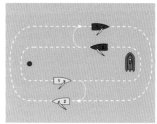

Option 1

Option 2

Option 2 (see illustration) removes spreader mark so fleet must maintain the shape of the circle. The whistle signals a change in direction turning in towards the coach boat thus making the circle smaller each time. As the game continues the circle becomes tighter and the whistles closer together.

Aim
• Improves boat handling.
• Fun with an element of competition.

Set up – Start by briefing the boats and then line them up behind the coach boat on starboard tack in 'follow my leader' formation. On the first whistle the coach boat will stop and the fleet will start to circle the boat clockwise. Make sure the circle is large enough for there to be a minimum of 3 boat lengths between each boat. On the next whistle the boats will change direction turning towards the coach boat thus making the circle slightly smaller. Boats will now be circling anti-clockwise and the exercise is repeated. Continue the exercise until the circle is too small for the ability of the group and then re-start.

Variations – Try a version of this exercise where you can eliminate the boat in front by overtaking them. You can only eliminate a boat if you overtake around the outside of the circle therefore preventing people cutting corners.

Coaching Points
• Start Keep it simple, focus on the 5 Essentials and where overtaking took place.
• Intermediate Getting the boat up to speed quickly out of the tack is a great way to gain on the boat in front.

Trim Tabs (1+boats)

START INTERMEDIATE

Gear – Coach boat or training partner.

Description – A self-grading exercise to highlight correct boat balance and trim. Start by sailing upwind with the boat perfectly upright and a coach or partner following behind. One boat sails to windward with a shadowing boat grading them out of ten on the accuracy and consistency of boat balance during a minute of sailing including gusts and lulls.

Aim
- Understand the feeling of when a boat is upright, heeled to windward or to leeward and how this impacts speed and steerage.

Set up – Sail to windward with the shadow boat directly behind for one minute. If sailing with a training partner swap roles and repeat.

Variations – Target an angle of 5° windward heel upwind and repeat the process downwind. Then discuss the relative feel and behaviour of the boat.

Coaching Points
- Start Try to link the feel of the boat to rig theory and loop this back into setting up for gusts and lulls. Revisit the exercise asking the sailors to be proactive rather than reactive to changes in pressure.

Tethered Rudders

Gear – Thick elastic for every boat in the group, buoys as required.

Description – A variation on rudderless sailing using elastic to maintain a neutral helm. Tie the elastic from the tiller to a fixed point on the centre line, then try to sail a set course while becoming less reliant on the tiller for steerage.

Aim
- Block off the rudder requiring the sailors to use sail trim and balance to steer the boat.
- Reduce the amount of rudder used by the helm.
- Develop a neutrally balanced boat.

Set up – Start with straight line sailing, tacking, gybing and slow speed manoeuvring without holding the tiller, then a simple course and finally put into a race situation.

Adaptation – Try reducing the tension on the elastic and sailing as normal. This allows sailors to appreciate the braking effect of the rudder through the resistance on the elastic. Use in conjunction with whistle exercises to train out over-steering.

Coaching Points
- Start During the briefing introduce the theory behind the balance point in the rig and how it impacts steerage. Highlight the effects of sail trim and boat balance while heading up, bearing away, tacking, gybing and when sailing in gusts and lulls.
- Intermediate Trying to emphasis the set-up for the turn is critical to making small rudder movements effective. Video the boats performing the exercise well, and assess their heel and sail trim on the entry to each manoeuvre.

Eyes shut sailing (1+boats)

INTERMEDIATE **ADVANCED**

Gear – 2-4 marks.

Description – The aim of this exercise is enhance feel by sailing unsighted, by getting one sailor at a time to close their eyes and feel the boat balance, boat speed and wind strength with their other senses. Crew must then feed-back the positions of other boats and obstructions.

Aim
- Enhance automatic sailing skills.
- Train out visual dominance and heighten other senses.
- Reinforce the importance of communication.

Set up – Using a course of your choice, brief the sailors on the rules and decide who will sail blind first (helm or crew). Start the fleet individually at 10 second intervals with sailors able to open their eyes at any point if they become uncomfortable. The aim is for sailors to increase the time they spend with their eyes closed.

Top Tip
Give the teams an 'eyes open' word for dangerous situations that may lead to collisions. Ensure the course is laid well away from others.
For single handers use 10 seconds eyes closed at a time or have boats sail in pairs with just one helm having his eyes closed at any one time.

Coaching Points
- Intermediate Helps train crews to provide better input on the race course improving timing and content.
- Advanced Your eyes are the least effective sense for judging boat speed. Your sense of balance is better with your eyes shut. The more you learn to feel the correct angle to the wind the less reliant you will become at using the telltales. So what do we need our eyes for?

Diamond Winger (2+boats)   INTERMEDIATE **ADVANCED**

Gear – 4 marks and a coach boat.

Description – Similar to the Gut Buster (see page 21) but less exhausting! After the gate is open the boats should sail on starboard (early starters may require a double tack) to gybe around Mark 1 to port. Mark 2 is effectively a port approach requiring a tack gybe before heading to Mark 3. This is a simple gybe to starboard before rounding the coach boat to port again.

Aim
- Create unfamiliar mark rounding situations.
- Include as many different manoeuvres as possible.

Set up – Lay 3 marks in an inverted V and position the coach boat to form a diamond course. Start the exercise with a gate start, the pathfinder ducking the start boat to open the gate. Use a hook finish at the start boat to end the exercise.

Variations – For a simpler version of this course, set a smaller diamond and set individual boats off at 30 second intervals from the coach boat.

Coaching Points
- Intermediate Try to get sailors to focus on routines for each manoeuvre. Pay particular attention to a tight exit on Mark 1 and the difficult port approach gybe set on Mark 2. When sailing in a fleet think ahead and prepare for possible attacking and defending opportunities while rounding marks.

Tack and Duck (2+boats)   INTERMEDIATE **ADVANCED**

Gear – None.

Description – Simulates crossing opportunities and close contact ducking. Start with boats on starboard tack, close hauled with leeward boats slightly bow out. As soon as possible the bottom (leeward) boat must tack and then duck the boat on their hip. They must then tack back onto starboard to become the new holding boat. If using more than two boats the 'ducker' may choose to cross boats but must always duck the top (furthest starboard) boat to ensure the exercise maintains its shape. Once a boat becomes the most leeward boat they must tack as soon as possible and the exercise keeps rolling.

Aim
- Practise generating space to tack, reducing preparation time before bearing away and judging crossing opportunities.

Set Up – Line up on starboard tack in a tuning run pattern. Possibly use a rabbit start to line everyone up.

Variations – Vary the focus by placing more emphasis on crossing rather than ducking boats and vice versa. You can use it to simulate lanes where you are trying to get an opportunity to cross or where you are being held out i.e. port lay lines or directly after starting.

Coaching Points
- Intermediate Try to force 'duckers' to be proactive in generating gaps to duck or cross the 'holding' boat. This will reduce the lead in time, speed up the whole exercise and increase the difficulty.
- Advanced Pinching prior to the duck will help protect your lane if you have boats to leeward ducking the same starboard tacker.

Hot Pursuit   INTERMEDIATE **ADVANCED**

Gear – 4 marks (fixed or unfixed) and 2 boats.

Description – A cross between "follow my leader" and match racing with one boat shadowing its partner while keeping the gap to a minimum. The lead boat must stay within a preset area but can sail any course they wish for 3 minutes. The boats then switch places and repeat the exercise.

Aim
- Improve boat handling routines.
- Reduce the time taken to react to other boats by better communication.

Set up – Lay 4 or more buoys in close proximity either in a square or at random.

Variations – Introduce a rule that allows the chase boat to win the match by overtaking the lead boat thus scoring a point. The lead boat wins a match by leading for the full 3 minutes with the first to 3 points winning the tie.

Coaching Points
- Intermediate Pinpoint the area where the biggest comparative gains or losses are made by using the relative distance between the two boats. Then compare techniques and discuss where improvements can be made.
- Advanced Focus on boats that fall out of set routines when pressure is applied. Use the video to analyse why this occurred.

Gut Buster (3+boats)   INTERMEDIATE **ADVANCED**

Gear – Coach boat and 2 marks.

Description – (see illustration) After the start, boats must complete a minimum of 4 tacks before reaching the coach boat at the midpoint. They must then perform a 360° around the coach boat to port (completing the tack) then perform another 4 tacks before the windward mark. After the top mark they will need to do a minimum of 3 gybes before dropping the kite and doing a 360° around the coach boat again. After re-hoisting they will need to do 3 more gybes before rounding the leeward mark to starboard and completing one lap.

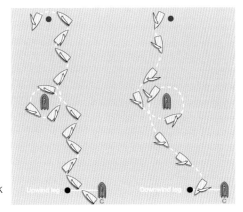

Aim
- Fitness.
- Boat handling and penalty practice.
- Compresses the fleet together, increasing pressure and forcing mistakes.

Set up – Lay a short course with a single leeward mark. Position the coach boat at the starboard end of the start line and run a 3 minute sequence. After the gun, motor up to the mid-point of the course and hold position as the middle mark.

Variations – Use a 30 second interval between starters with the aim being to overtake the boat in front. Sailing boats individually will mean the exercise is process driven, working towards performing the manoeuvres well. In a race situation the emphasis will be on tactics and boat handling under pressure.

Top Tips
For lower ability groups try setting boats off individually at 30 second intervals. Moving the coach boat further up the course for the first 360° will also give the fleet time to settle.

Coaching Points
- Intermediate A common fault is to rush the exercise and put teamwork under even more pressure. Throwing routines out of the window when boats meet is a symptom of panic decisions.
- Advanced Re-focus the sailors on the 5 Essentials as they become more able to cope with the pressure of the exercise.

The 'V' Trail (2+boats)   INTERMEDIATE **ADVANCED**

Gear – coach boat, red and green flags.

Description – Boats set off at 30 second intervals, in a pair or in groups of 3. They will then round left windward mark, coach boat, right windward mark in that order. All windward marks to be rounded to port, with the coach indicating the leeward rounding using red and green flags. Boats will continue to sail the course until they hear repeated whistles when rounding the coach boat.

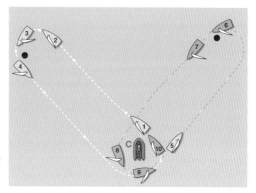

Aim
• Rehearse and refine every type of mark rounding in a pressure environment.
• Can also be used as an overtaking drill based on winning overlaps on the approach to a mark.
• Simulates a heavily biased leeward mark rounding involving a 270° turn.

Set up – Lay 2 windward marks 2-3 hundred metres apart. Position the coach boat midway between the two marks approximately 100 metres to leeward. The coach boat will become the leeward mark but can remain mobile. A good tip when setting the coach boat position is to get a boat to sail on the lay line to each mark then re-set near the lay lines.

Variations – This works really well as an elimination series with heats determining a final of three boats. To start, get the boats to circle the coach boat and release them when you deem it fair. Only the lead boat progresses to the final although alternative formats can be used depending on group size.

Top Tip
Make the sailors work. If they can still talk after this one then the course is too short!

Coaching Points
• Intermediate Sailors need to remain flexible with downwind angle. When debriefing, discuss shifting from soak mode to fully arced up!
• Advanced Think ahead about gaining the overlap for the next mark rounding. Like chess, the move might be set-up some time before, in this case at the previous mark rounding.

Slow Speed Control

Slow speed training is a key element of good starting and also highlights the key skills required to control the boat without the rudder. Don't forget that trim and balance all work in opposite ways when going astern as well as rudder control. These exercises are excellent for developing a thorough understanding of the essentials of boat handling.

Top Tip
In a 2 man boat make sure that there is continuous communication between the helm and crew.

Holding Station (1 boat)

START INTERMEDIATE

Gear – 1 mark.

"That's 30 seconds!"

Description – This is a simple boat handling exercise which requires a boat to sail up next to a mark and hold position on starboard tack for as long as possible. Sailor/sailors are required to hold the boat stationary minimising slippage and fore and aft movement. The timer starts when the boat takes up a position next to the mark and finishes when the drift is beyond a pre-determined distance.

Aim
- Introduce the concept of slippage.
- Improve slow speed boat handling.
- Simulate holding a position on a start line.

Set up – None.

Variation – Use different approaches, for example from behind, reaching in from above and tacking in from underneath. Add acceleration into the exercise by getting boats to hold position until the whistle is blown, the boats must then accelerate to max speed.

Coaching Points
- Start Get the sailors to try to minimise slippage. With different approaches highlight how the boat carries momentum and how this affects your approach up to the mark.

The Drive Through (1+boats)

INTERMEDIATE

Gear – coach boat.

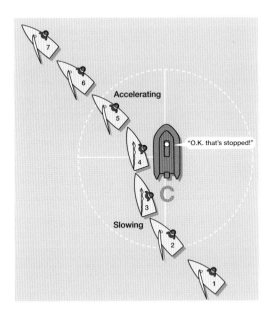

Description – The aim of the game is for the focus boat to sail into the 'drive though', come to a dead stop next to the coach boat, and then accelerate out as fast as possible (within the rules). When one boat clears the circle the next boat can start. The advantage of this drill is that the coach can provide instant feedback while the boat is in the circle.

Aim
- Fun, fast and multi-skilled.
- Teaches rapid changes in speed.
- Can be applied to starting situations.

Set up – When running this drill with more than one boat get the fleet to hold position in a line outside a 3-6 boat length circle. When a boat exits the drive through the next boat can start. Once a boat exits the drive through they re-join the end of the queue for seconds.

Coaching Points
- Intermediate Here we are focused on cutting time and distance to full stop and time and distance to max speed. Video each boat individually and comment on the radius of the imaginary circle.

Reverse Park (1 boat)

INTERMEDIATE **ADVANCED**

Gear – 1 mark.

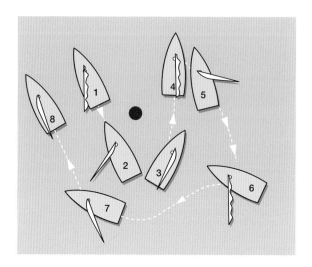

Description – Start by holding position next to a mark on starboard tack. Initiate and control a reverse staying as close to the mark as possible before exiting on port. Sheet on and sail forward so you are next to the mark and stop. Hold position before doing the same process in reverse.

Aim
- Slow speed boat handling.
- Simulate moving in and out of position on the starting line.
- Excellent for communication in two-man boats.

Set Up – None.

Variations – Try performing the same exercise without initiating the reverse therefore retaining right of way. Shift the emphasis from staying close to the mark to speed from start position to end position.

Coaching Points
- Intermediate Look at using the sails to initiate and assist the reverse. Backing will have a different effect from one side to the other.
- Advanced Control is fundamental when reversing. Getting the bow at the right angle to the wind before backing the main will result in more consistent changes in direction. Boat balance will also affect the direction a boat will want to reverse so highlight this in the debrief.

Acceleration

Slow speed skills are useless if you can't accelerate off the start line. This section deals with how to achieve that speed.

Trigger Pull (2+boats)

Gear – coach boat.

Description – The name of the game is to have the best acceleration in the fleet. To test this all boats must be level before putting the pedal to the metal. There is a 1 minute rolling sequence for this exercise so: the first gun is to line up, the second go and the third stop. All boats should agree a time they will start to accelerate, for example 6 seconds. At this point they should still be together as it's the bit after we are interested in. Once started the boats try to hold their lane until the next gun.

"So, when I say 'GO', go for it"

Aim
- Practise the process of acceleration.
- Get used to holding lanes.
- Get as many starts in as possible with minimum set up time.

Set Up – Start by getting the group to line up warning them before the first signal. Move the coach boat to windward so the sailors have a reference point and then sound 1 minute. Keep the fleet in line by giving instructions and then video the start giving feedback after each cycle. It's essential to get the slower boats repositioned quickly and not disrupt the exercise.

Variations – Lower ability groups can form a line behind the coach boat. On the first signal boats must harden up onto a close hauled course and have their sails flapping. On the second signal they all accelerate. On the third signal they stop. Try moving boats around after every start removing any positional advantage.

Coaching Points
- Intermediate Compare individual techniques and discuss which are most effective in terms of time to max speed and height lost.
- Advanced Get boats to use a holding position closer to head to wind. Try changing the trigger time to 3 seconds to simulate being on transit and unable to go too early.

Time to the Max (1+boats)

START INTERMEDIATE

Gear – 2 marks, coach boat and video camera.

Description – At 1 minute the focus boat enters the start area and holds position on the line. At the gun the boat accelerates to maximum speed at which point the crew raises a hand. The name of the game is to reach maximum speed as quickly as possible from a standing start.

Aim
- Practise acceleration skills.
- Create an awareness of the time needed to reach full speed.
- Reduce time taken to reach maximum speed.

Set up – Lay 2 marks 3 boat lengths apart and square to the wind. Set the coach boat up to leeward of the line and start a 3 minute rolling-clock. Give signals at 3, 1, and go. On the gun follow the focus boat until they reach full speed then return back to the line. The next boat enters the line on the following 1 minute signal.

Variations – Get the sailors to start with different amounts of flow and the foils to highlight the effect on acceleration. Try moving forward slightly, completely stationary and with slight sternway.

Coaching Points
- Start Focus on consistency, roles in the boat and sail controls.
- Intermediate Compare relative techniques trying to reduce time to optimum speed.

Out of the Blocks (2+boats)   START INTERMEDIATE

Gear – 1 mark, coach boat.

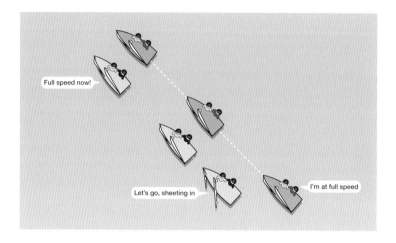

Description – A paired starting exercise with one boat taking a timed run to the start line and the other starting from stationary holding position 2 boat lengths behind the line. The boats will then continue to race until one has a clear advantage.

Aim
- Improve time and distance skill.
- Develop acceleration skills of stationary boat.

Set up – Lay a square line long enough for two boats. Run a rolling 3 minute sequence. Select one boat to make a 30 second timed run into the start with the other holding position at two boat lengths. After each start get boats to switch positions.

Variations – This exercise can be run with more boats on the line taking a similar format to 'hoverers and hunters' (see page 38).

Coaching Points
- Start Focus on the skill of timed approaches. Get sailors to practise their run so that they can hit the line at full speed.
- Intermediate Compare relative techniques trying to reduce time to optimum speed.

Line Starts

The next stage of skill development is applying them in a real situation. This section looks at testing those starting skills and introducing the tactical considerations of one of the most important sections of the race.

Getting off the line in the front row is probably the most important skill in racing. It then gives you the option to sail where you want as opposed to being controlled by the fleet, learning how to get in the front row and then how to accelerate quickly is invaluable.

Line Starts (2+boats)   START INTERMEDIATE

Gear – 1 mark, coach boat and visual signals (battens, flags or hand signals).

Description – The start is a fundamental aspect of sailboat racing. This basic exercise can be used at every level to test a variety of skills. There are several options for starting sequences. 5, 4, 1, Go! 3, 2, 1, Go! Or simply 2 minute rolling starts.

Aim
- An opportunity to practise all aspects of starting from taking transits, to slow speed boat handling and accelerating.

Set Up – Lay a start line of a length relative to the ability and size of group.

Variations – Depending on the type of start you are focusing on, you may choose to lay an even line or one with a port or starboard end bias. The length of line also depends on the focus of the drill. Shorter lines test slow-speed boat handling and longer lines shift the focus onto positioning, approaches and acceleration.

Coaching Points
- Start Looking at identifying possible weak areas in the groups starting which can then be addressed using more specific exercises. Try giving the better starters in the group set positions or approaches. This will handicap them while retaining a positive outcome from the exercise.

Bias Basics (1+boats)   START

Gear – Pin end and coach boat.

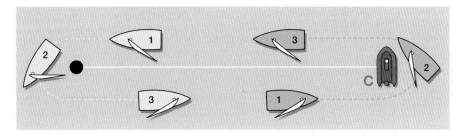

Description – Musical chairs on water. Sailors need to sail around the start line leaving the ends to port. By keeping the sails set after tacking round the starboard end they will be able to tell if they are sailing towards or away from the favoured end. When the coach blows the whistle they need to sail to the favoured end as fast as possible. Fastest boat to the correct end wins.

Aim
- Good introduction to line bias.
- Gets sailors to use the RYA technique for assessing bias.
- Adds an element of competition to the exercise.

Set up – Start with a 10° bias to the starboard end and shift the bias to the pin for the second start. As the fleet gets better at selecting the correct end of the line, make the line squarer to the wind and reduce the time between whistles – like stopping the music in musical chairs!

Variation – Try turning the drill into a competition with one boat eliminated each round until you get a two boat final. Make the line less biased each time and add an additional exercise so the fleet cannot cheat by watching you re-lay the line.

Coaching Points
- Start Get the sailors to comment on why some lines are easier to judge than others? Discuss different methods of checking bias and their relative merits.

Rabbit Starts (3+boats)   START INTERMEDIATE

Gear – Ideally a start mark although it's not essential.

Description – This is basically a gate start without the fuss. The 'rabbit' or 'pathfinder' sets off at a preset time (either using repeated whistles when they start their run or after a timed sequence). This effectively opens the gate allowing the boats to start by ducking his or her stern. When all boats have crossed the line the 'rabbit' can tack on top of the fleet closing the gate.

I'm the rabbit

Aim
- Take the emphasis away from the start by giving all boats a potentially clear lane.
- Keep the fleet together when starting exercises.
- Help improve judging closing speeds and approach lay lines.

Set Up
- Identify the 'rabbit' and get them to sail on port.
- All boats must duck the 'rabbit' on starboard tack and then harden up onto a close-hauled course. The 'rabbit' can tack back onto starboard when all boats have started, effectively closing the gate.
- When one boat is clear ahead the fleet should stop and reposition for the next start.

Variations – The options here are what to do with the fleet after the start. You can use the exercise as a means of starting a race or tuning run or simply recall the fleet when one boat has sailed over or crossed all the other boats.

Top Tip
When running this exercise for the first time use the coach boat as a guard boat to protect the 'rabbit' from frisky starters.

Coaching Points
- Start Time and distance. Judge the speed of the 'rabbit' and decide where from and when to accelerate from so you can cross behind on close-hauled course at maximum speed. Focus on boats that had a poor exit from the 'rabbit' and decide if that was due to speed, poor judgement or being boxed in.
- Intermediate Tactically it's about positioning and deciding whether you want to exit the gate early or late. Ask the sailors what the benefits would be and why?

30 + 30 (2+boats)

START INTERMEDIATE

Gear – 1 mark and coach boat.

Description – The name of the game is to be on the line with 30 seconds to go and prepared for the gun to go at any time between 30 seconds before start time and 30 seconds after start time. Boats must hold position and then respond to the gun with the winner being the boat clear ahead when the start is recalled.

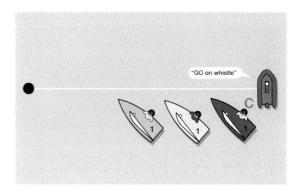

"GO on whistle"

Aim
- Get the fleet up onto the line good and early.
- Improve boat control.
- Help improve acceleration from a standstill.
- Respond to external start cues.

Set up – First lay a square line of an adequate length for the fleet to get a clear start or slightly shorter. Use a 3,1, GO sequence and fire the GO when you feel the time is right. Go early if the fleet is late in lining up or late if they look to be too close to the line. Use a round the ends rule and disqualify anyone who is over and does not go back.

Variations – Try the exercise with different line bias to reinforce the need to get in early or get the approach transit right.

Coaching Points
- Start Get them on the line early, push sailors to get a front row start even if their boat handling isn't up to it.
- Intermediate Link the skill of responding to the whistle by going when the boat to windward accelerates. These external cues call for good awareness and reactions and having the boat ready to accelerate and not stationary.

Box Starts (2+boats)   START INTERMEDIATE

Gear – 3 marks, optional windward mark, and start boat.

Description – The rules of the exercise are that all boats must be within the box formed by the marks and the start boat from a pre-determined time. Any boats sailing outside the box during this period will be disqualified. To finish the exercise you can recall the fleet after 1 minute, wait until one boat is clear ahead or use a windward mark and finish at the start line.

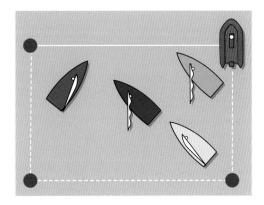

Aim
- Compress boats into a smaller area simulating larger fleets.
- Put an emphasis on slow-speed boat handling.
- Encourage boats to start from a stationary holding position, improving acceleration.

Set Up – Set the line square to the wind of suitable length so that all boats can fit comfortably on the line. Lay 2 additional marks, downwind of the pin and the start boat. This forms a box the size of which is dictated by the ability of the group and the class of dinghy.

Variations – As the ability of the group improves bring the two box marks up towards the start line increasing the difficulty. Moving one box mark is also a good variation as this can simulate less room to manoeuvre at one end of the line. Varying the time that the box is closed is another option. The more time in the box – the harder the exercise.

Coaching Points
- Start Get boats to sit out and watch if they find the boat control difficult.
- Intermediate Be assertive with penalties so the fleet adheres to the rules correctly!

Port Tack Players (3+boats)

INTERMEDIATE

Gear – Pin end and a coach boat.

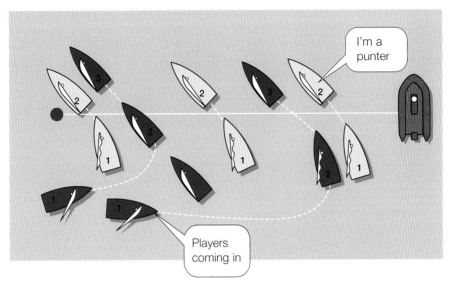

Description – Split the fleet into port tack 'players' and starboard tack 'punters'. The 'punters' must be on the line with 2 minutes to go with the players released at 1 minute from the pin. Players can either start early, tacking into a gap to start on starboard, or time their run to port tack the start at some point along the line. The start can either be recalled or the fleet can race to the windward mark before finishing at the start-finish line.

Aim
- Practise different port attack approaches.
- Teach starboard tack boats to defend their gaps.
- Improve boat handling, time, distance and acceleration.

Set-up – Start with a square line with enough room for the fleet to get a clean start. Decide on who's who and then run two starts, one even and one biased then switching over roles.

Variations: Release the 'punters' at 15 seconds from the pin to cut out the tacking option.

Coaching Points
- Intermediate Encourage sailors to use different approaches to develop a variety of starting options and their strategic impact in the race.

Hoverers & Hunters (3+boats)   INTERMEDIATE ADVANCED

Gear – 1 mark and coach boat.

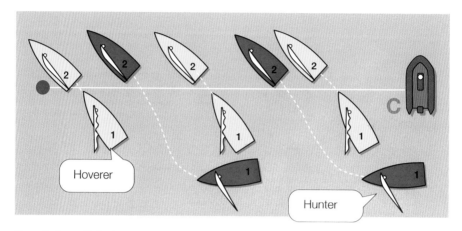

Description – Split the fleet into 'hoverers' and 'hunters'. The 'hoverers' must get onto the line at 1 minute and then hold position until start time. The 'hunters' must enter the line in the final 30 seconds, ideally hitting the line at max speed. The 'hoverers' may block the 'hunters' from entering the line but they must do so within the rules. The exercise continues until one boat is clear ahead or tacks and crosses the fleet.

Aim
- Simulate late approaches onto the line and helps sailors to recognise gaps on the line with potential and those that are high risk.
- Practice for attacking and defending strategies on the line.

Set up – Start with a square line with enough room for the fleet to get a clean start. Decide on who's who and then run two starts, one even and one biased before switching over roles.

Variations – Change the rules so 'hoverers' cannot drop their bow past close-hauled and the 'hunters' cannot slow down after they pull the trigger. This shifts the emphasis onto acceleration for the 'hoverers' and time and distance for the 'hunters'.

Coaching Points
- Intermediate Video the starts and assess safe and high risk approaches and highlight alternatives.
- Advanced Look at defending and attacking options.

Reverse Traverse (3+boats)

Gear – 1 mark and start boat.

Description – Starting at the start boat end, get all boats to hold position approximately 1 boat width apart. On the first whistle get the top boat to reverse out of line and sail behind the other boats before lining up again as the leeward boat. The next whistle can then be blown, signalling the new top boat to exit the line and the process is repeated.

Aim
- Simulate repositioning on the start line.
- Good boat handling practice.

Set up – Lay a square line approximately 50 metres in length. Signal the fleet to line up at the starboard end and when happy with the positioning start the drill.

Variation – The exercise can be repeated in the opposite direction by getting the top boat to double tack up the line with each boat doing the same on subsequent whistles. Mix the exercise up so one signal means move up and the other move down.

Coaching Points
- Start Ensure boats by correctly keeping clear avoid infringing. Video boat control when initiating the reverse.
- Intermediate Place and emphasise the speed of manoeuvring, emphasise teamwork, sail trim and boat balance to improve control.

Mystery Mark (3+boats)   ~~INTERMEDIATE~~ ADVANCED

Gear – 2-3 marks & coach boat.

Description – Lay a
starting line with two
marks at the port end.
The idea is that mark
1 should provide a
starboard end biased
line with mark 2
favouring the port end.
At the 1 minute, or with
30 seconds till start
time, announce which
mark will be the pin

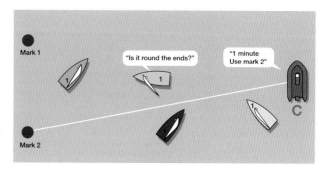

end of the line. This will require the fleet to reposition to take account of the line bias.
The race will then start under standard rules and can be recalled or finished using a
windward / leeward course finishing at the start line. If using the recall option, let the
fleet go until one boat has either crossed the fleet or is clear ahead.

Aim
- A great exercise for encouraging flexibility in starting.
- Sailors must make the best of given starting situation.
- Simulate starting in shifty conditions and can also simulate repositioning
  when losing a space on the line.

Set up – When first running this exercise try to lay two lines with a 10° bias in either
direction. This gives enough separation to clearly define each line. Make the line long
enough so there is sufficient room for manoeuvring and starting for the entire fleet. If the
line becomes overly biased to one mark, simply reposition the start boat.

Variations – Try changing the time boats have to reposition from 1 minute to 30
seconds. You may also say that the end of the line you choose prior to revealing the
pin, is the end you must start from. This will reinforce the skills of starting from an
unfavoured end.

Top Tip
Try to video attacking and defending scenarios that occur during the final
30 seconds.

Coaching Points
- Intermediate Decisive decision making and awareness are skills required for
  reposition prestart.
- Advanced What's the best re-positioning solution? Risk and reward?

Private Gate (3+boats)　　　START INTERMEDIATE

Gear – 3 marks, optional windward mark and start boat.

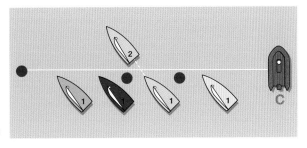

Description – The rules of this exercise are pretty simple. Two extra marks are laid on the start line and one boat is nominated as the 'gate keeper'. Only they can start between these marks, all other boats must start in the free areas either side of the gate. The start can then be recalled once there is a clear winner or after rounding a windward mark and returning to the start / finish line.

Aim
- Focus on one boat.
- Give them the opportunity to have a clear start.
- Practise planning approaches to set positions on the line.

Set Up – Lay a line long enough there is sufficient room for the fleet to get a clear start. Position two marks in the middle of the line 1 boat length apart, these can either be on the line or if you do not want them to act as line sights lay them a boat length behind.

Variations – By shifting the position of the gate towards the favoured end you can ensure the 'gate keeper' gets an even better start. Alternatively increase the difficulty of the exercise by getting the free boats to try and use the rules to block the 'gate keeper' from getting to their position on the line. This could be given a competitive element by awarding 1 point to the 'gate keeper' for starting in the gate, 2 points for winning the start from the gate and 1 point to the fleet if the 'gate keeper' is blocked out. The highest scorer after a full rotation wins.

Top Tip
Adapt the gate to the skill level of the individual. Try and turn it into a personal handicap system making it easier for less able sailors.

Coaching Points
- Start Focus on approach transits.

Block the Barger (3+boats)   ~~INTERMEDIATE~~ ADVANCED

Gear – 3 marks and start boat.

Description – One boat is elected the 'lay-line legend'. At the 2 minute signal, it must enter the start area from the approach marker and must try to win the start boat. The remaining boats must remain to the right of the start boat until the 'legend' has entered the start area. At this point they must pass between the start boat and the approach mark with the aim being to get the best start possible.

Aim
- Reinforces the importance of approach transits.
- Highlight options for boats high of the approach transit.
- Attacking and defending strategies.
- Rule observance.

Set up – Lay a start line long enough for the entire fleet and lay an approach mark on the start boat's starboard lay-line 25-30 metres down. Get a boat to sail on close-hauled up to the start boat to assist in laying this mark. Either lay a windward mark 100 metres to windward or recall the start. Ideally each boat must have a chance to play the 'legend', recalls may be a better option for larger groups. The sequence is 3, 2, 1, GO. Repeat selecting a new 'legend' either by rotation or as the last boat in each race.

Variations – Moving the approach mark will tend to spread out or compress 'bargers' making the exercise easier or more difficult. Also try varying the time the 'bargers' are allowed to enter the start area.

Coaching Points
- Intermediate Highlight how getting the starboard transit right will improve defending options. Also reinforce the options for boats high of the approach line.
- Advanced All about predicting the actions of others. Seeing scenarios before they occur and pre-empting them.

Sequential Starts (3+boats) START INTERMEDIATE ADVANCED

Gear – 1 mark and a start boat.

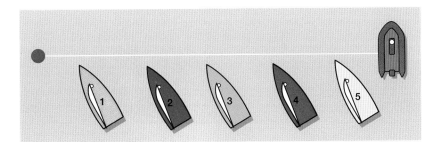

Description – Give each member of the group a number, position number 1 at the pin end and the highest number closest to the start boat. The fleet must start in sequence, any boat out of position at start time is disqualified. The winner is the first boat to cross or sail over the fleet. Once the start has been won the boats can return to the line to re-start the sequence. Each boat must now move one place down the line with the bottom boat moving up to start next to the start boat.

Aim
- Practise starting out of position.
- Change gear to suit your starting position relative to the fleet or bias.
- Reinforce the importance of flexibility in starting.

Set Up – Start by laying a square line, long enough for the fleet to get a clear start. Ensure you perform one complete cycle with all boats starting from all positions with an unbiased line.

Variations – This start is best used for practising biased line starts. The bias must remain the same for one complete cycle. Try pin or start boat favoured lines but remember the greater the bias the smaller lanes become so be aware of the group's ability.

Coaching Points
- Start There's more than one place to start. Get sailors to discuss how this might affect their starting in big fleets.
- Intermediate Reinforce the need to change gear relative to their position on the fleet and the line bias. Going for height or speed at the right time will be the difference between winning and losing the start.
- Advanced The greater the bias the smaller the lanes so lane management and generating or defending space pre-start is critical.

Sailing to Windward

The better the group understands the rules and set up of the exercises covered in this section the more effective they will become. The best way to achieve this is to use 'walk through' simulations on shore and only progress on to the water once all sailors understand what is expected of them.

Beat Bias (3+boats)

Gear – 2 marks and a coach boat.

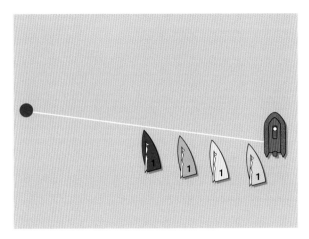

Description – The rules are simple, start, race to the windward mark, round it to port and return to the finish.

Aim
- Introduce course bias to strategy.
- Require sailors to change modes of sailing to suit individual lanes.
- Establish the favoured end may not be the best place to start.

Set up – Start with a square line, with the windward mark 200 metres to windward and 20° to the left of the true wind direction. Run a 3, 1, GO, start sequence and then finish the race at the start/finish line before re-setting and going back into the sequence.

Variations – Try setting the course with the course biased to port and the line to starboard and vice versa.

Coaching Points
- Start Reinforce how the sailors that reached the windward mark first may not have started at the favoured end of the line. Ask question as to why this is the case.
- Intermediate Be aware of tacking options before you get too close to lay lines. Show how a port bias course becomes congested on the port lay line and that a starboard bias tends to cause the fleet to over-stand the starboard lay line as boats search for clear lanes.

Lay-ed Back (2+boats)   START

Gear – 2 marks and coach boat.

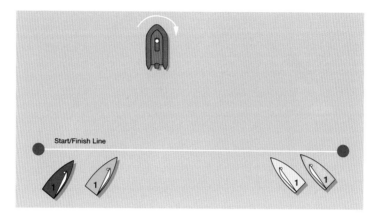

Description – Boats must line up between the two start marks on either the port lay for the coach boat or the starboard lay. At a preset start time boats sail towards the coach boat looking to round to port and return to the start/finish line. Boats must observe the racing rules and aim to be first home. Boats then rotate to the opposite lay line and repeat the exercise.

Aim
- Judging lay lines.
- Pro-active decision making when boats meet.
- Rules.
- Simulate championship windward marks rounding.

Set up – Lay 2 marks approximately 100 metres apart. Allocate a lay line to each member of the group and start a rolling 3 minute timer. Motor 50 metres to windward in the middle of the course and hold position. Video the boats as they approach and comment on situations as they occur.

Variations – Moving the coach boat to port or starboard will shift the advantage to one lay line changing the scenario. By moving further to windward you can make all the boats tack and create new situations and outcomes.

Coaching Points
- Start Look around, communicate in the boat and think ahead.
- Intermediate Look at changing your mode of sailing when crossing or ducking boats.

Cross the Centre Line (1+boats)

Gear – 2 marks and a coach boat.

Description – This exercise is to get over to the centre line of the course as soon as possible after starting and to then sail up the middle of the course crossing the centre line as many times as possible before the windward mark. The boat that crosses the centre line most is deemed the winner.

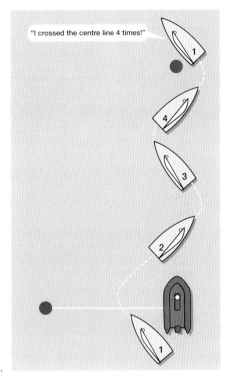

"I crossed the centre line 4 times!"

Aim
- Reinforce the benefits of sailing on the middle of the course.
- Improve awareness of course position relative to the centre line.
- Stop sailors hitting lay lines too early.

Set up – Lay a square start line with a windward mark positioned with 5-10 degrees starboard bias. Send boats off the line at 10 second intervals, each boat remembering the number of times they crossed the centre line. Once you have completed a complete cycle, relay the windward mark with a port bias and repeat.

Variations – Try running the exercise as a race with a line start. Assign all boats a minimum number of times they have to cross the centre line upwind and downwind. The winner is the first boat to cross the start/finish line.

The Channel (2+boats)

Gear – 2 coach boats.

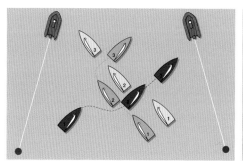 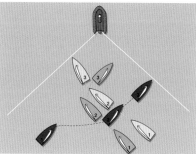

Description – This uses the coach boat to dictate an area the fleet can sail within. The imaginary lines extending behind the coach boat may not be crossed, the idea being that the exercise increases in difficulty the further you progress up the course.

Aim
- Simulates larger fleets.
- Force boats into close crossing situations.
- Introduce rules when boats meet.
- An element of momentum as the exercise gets harder the further the sailor's progress.

Set up – Start with a 'follow my leader' on starboard tack reaching behind the left hand coach boat. On the first whistle the fleet hardens up and sails on a close-hauled course to windward. The two coach boats then motor parallel to each other for several minutes. When the fleet has settled get the left hand coach to take a slightly converging course and increase the difficulty.

Variations – Option 1: Use one coach boat with imaginary banks extending 45° out from each back quarter.
Option 2: Requires two coach boats with the line of the bank extending out from the centre line of each coach boat.

Coaching Points
- Start Get sailors to ask for room to tack when reaching a riverbank.
- Intermediate Get sailors to think ahead and try to overtake using the rules to their advantage.

Shift Simulator (3+boats) INTERMEDIATE **ADVANCED**

Gear – 3 marks, green and red flags and coach boat.

Description – Starts off as a normal start, then, at 1 minute the coach will signal to round the left or right windward mark. The first sailor to round the correct windward mark and cross the start/finish line is deemed the winner.

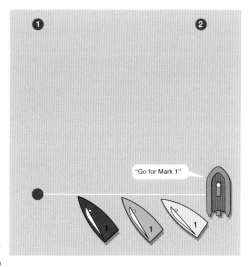

Aim
* Simulate a wind shift during the starting sequence.
* Encourage fast reposition when responding to a change on the course.

Set up – Lay start line long enough for the fleet to start plus a third. Motor upwind 100-200 metres and drop two windward marks 100 metres apart and square to the wind. Return to the starboard end of the line and start the sequence. At 1 minute hold up either the red or green flag. Video the fleet repositioning and provide feedback after each race and during the debrief.

Variations – Change the distance between windward marks and the length of course to shift the focus. Shorter courses with more separation are more about the start. Longer courses are about winning lanes and modes of sailing.

Coaching Points
* Intermediate Emphasise the time and opportunities boats have to re-position. Sometimes staying put and switching modes at start time can be more effective.
* Advanced Encourage boats to bank their lanes out of the line to secure an advantage or to open a tacking opportunity.

Mark Roundings

A key area to win and lose places is the mark rounding. These are a great set of exercises for raising tactical awareness and developing an understanding for the rules. The key to these exercises is to use the 'dinghy park shuffle' (see page 66) to demonstrate the realities of the rules and tactics in a slow time, three dimensional, learning environment.

Mini Course (2+boats) START

Gear – 1 mark and coach boat.

Description – Start following the coach boat on a beam reach. On the whistle harden up onto a close hauled course and race to the windward mark. Leaving the windward mark to port bear away and sail to the finish behind the coach boat.

Aim
- Keep the fleet together for the windward mark rounding.
- Right of way rules at congested mark rounding.
- Teach sailors safe and high risk approaches to the windward mark.

Set up – Use a 'follow my leader' exercise to get the group in a line directly behind the coach boat about 100 metres downwind of the windward mark. Release the fleet with a whistle and then hold position to act as the finish line.

Variations – Try setting the fleet off on both port and starboard tack. By sending the front of the queue to the back you can keep revolving the boats especially if you want to make the exercise easier or harder for certain boats. The same exercise can be used for downwind mark rounding requiring a similar set up and a leeward mark.

Coaching Points
- Start The earlier you get on a lay line, the less options you have. Approaching the mark on port carries a higher risk unless you are clear ahead. Pay attention to boats coming downwind on opposite tacks.

Rabbit Approach (3+boats)   INTERMEDIATE **ADVANCED**

Gear – 1 mark.

Description – This uses a 'rabbit start' relatively close to the windward mark. The 'rabbit' sets off when the fleet is ready and may only tack back when the entire fleet as started. The aim of the game is to sail the fastest route to the windward mark while taking into account the other boats.

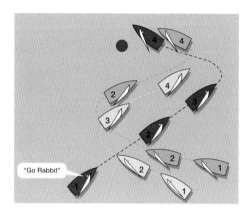

Aim
- Teach approach.
- Tactics.
- Keep the fleet close together.
- Create penalty situations.

Set up – For the first start, choose the 'rabbit' at random then ensure the 'rabbit' is the last boat from the previous race on all follow on races. Get the 'rabbit' to set off around 100-150 metres away from the windward mark depending on the conditions and class of dinghy. Set the 'rabbit' off directly downwind of the windward mark and finish the race when all boats have rounded the top mark. If you have a coach boat, use it to indicate the start position of the 'rabbit'.

Variations – Change the distance between the start and the top mark to spread the fleet out or bring them closer together. Also try adding the rule that the 'rabbit' must tack after the start to make sure they don't have too great an advantage.

Coaching Points
- Intermediate Do not wait for situations to get worse. If blocked out then make room to tack.
- Advanced Try to control the boats around you. Get the sailors to think about the threats and opportunities and how they can position themselves to take advantage of the situation.

Lay Lines

Lay lines are a significant factor when developing tactical awareness in sailors. These exercises help create real situations that may occur during racing.

Lay Line Crossover (1+boats)

START

Gear – 2 marks and a coach boat.

Description – Boats must duck the leeward mark on either port or starboard tack and one tack the beat. When they reach the mark they re-set and continue to the next mark on the opposite lay line. Boats judge their success by relative gains on their partner at each crossover. In general try not to get on to any lay line too early as any slight wind shift will mean that you lose places. In tidal situations do make sure that you are aware of the direction of the tide and how it is going to affect your approach to the mark.

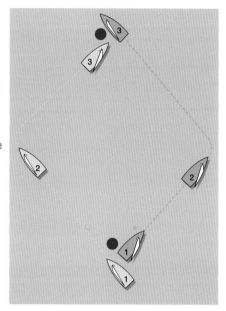

Aim
- Lay line practice.
- Exercise keeps rolling allowing maximum repetitions.
- Introduce the importance of clear lanes.

Set up – Lay 2 marks 50 metres apart. Return to the leeward mark and start the fleet off in pairs at 15 second intervals until all the boats have started. Pick up the leeward mark and re-lay as a new windward mark. Repeat.

Variations – Moving the marks further apart makes it harder to judge the lay line. Setting the fleet off together using a 'rabbit' start educates sailors to become more aware of clear lanes.

Coaching Points
- Start Try to encourage sailors to look back over their shoulder when judging lay lines. When a boat is ahead on the same lay line get the sailors to judge if they are high, low or bang-on and adjust their approach accordingly.

Zeb's Lay-Liner (1+boats)

Gear – 3 marks.

Description – A really good alternative
exercise for upwind and downwind lay
lines. Leaving all windward marks to
port, go starboard lay, port lay and then
starboard again. Round the top mark
and sail downwind to alternative lay lines.
Boats must aim to be within two boat
lengths of the lay line when approaching
on port.

Aim
- Upwind and downwind lay line
  practice.
- Simulate both port and starboard
  approaches.
- Can be shortened to include an
  element of boat handling.

Set up – Start by laying 3 marks in line
with the wind, approximately 50 metres
apart. Return to the leeward mark and set boats off at 30 second intervals.

Variations – Try running a pursuit race over 2 laps, setting boats off at 15 second
intervals. Less able sailors should be set off first with the speed merchants
starting later.

Coaching Points
- Intermediate Whenever you judge a lay line incorrectly, remember the error and
  make a correction the next time. Downwind try using a point on the boom as a
  sight for judging the lay.

Downwind Hopscotch (2+boats)

ADVANCED

Gear: 2 marks and a coach boat.

Description – A complicated exercise but a real beauty. It begins with a 'rabbit' start at Mark 1 with the 'rabbit' tack as soon as all the boats have started.

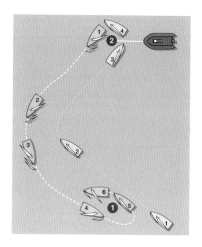

The boats then race to the windward mark, bear away and gybe on the port lay line. Meanwhile the coach picks up Mark 2 and re-sets downwind of Mark 1. The fleet will round Mark 1 to port and wait for the last boat, which will then act as a downwind 'rabbit' to restart the fleet by passing the mark to port. All boats then race downwind to the new leeward mark looking for an early gybe so as to approach the new mark on starboard lay and gybe drop. The race continues leaving the original mark to port, straight setting, sailing to the port lay and finishing with a straight drop to port. The last boat to finish becomes the 'rabbit' and the race is resailed.

Aim
- Lay line practice.
- Overtaking.
- Pressure boat handling.
- Keeps the fleet together.

Set up – Lay a windward leeward course approximately 200 metres apart depending on the conditions, class of dinghy and the ability of the group. Return to the leeward mark, pick a 'rabbit' and start a 3 minute sequence. Get the 'rabbit' to duck Mark 1 to start the race and then motor the coach boat upwind to Mark 2. When the last boat rounds the windward mark, pick it up and motor directly downwind 100 metres below Mark 1. Mark 2 is now the new leeward mark. Wait to finish the group and restart with the last boat from race 1 becoming the 'rabbit'.

Variations – Get the sailors to always gybe set at windward marks, and gybe drop at the leeward marks, passing them to port. Alternatively try alternate roundings on the downwind legs.

Coaching Points
- Advanced It's not just about lay lines, get sailors to think about generating the opportunity to gybe when overlapped or thinking about clear air after the gybe.

Downwind Sailing

Much of race training focuses on upwind speed and tactics and yet the biggest speed differences are downwind. This section helps the coach and sailors harness those skills for maximising downwind speed.

Downwind Flyer (1+boats)   START

Gear – Optional coach boat.

Description – Get sailors (helm and crew) to fix their positions in the boat so leverage remains the same. As pressure increases they can only steer to maintain boat balance, trimming for maximum speed. As pressure eases they must steer the correct amount to maintain a flat boat. Single whistles mean gybe, repeated whistles mean stop and line up behind the coach boat again.

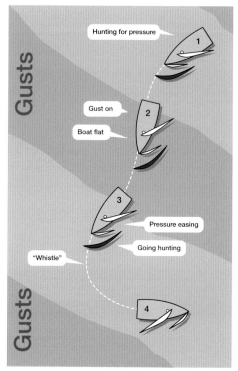

Aim
- Link steering to boat trim downwind and introduce apparent wind angle changes.
- Encourage sailors to be more aware of pressure over the course.

Set up – Start with the fleet reaching in a line on starboard about 3-4 boat lengths apart. On the whistle bear away (hoist) and sail downwind.

Variations – The same theory can be used for single-handed classes where heel dictates rudder balance, accurate steering results in less rudder use.

Coaching points
- Start Get the crew to feedback pressure information to the helm so the helm will be more accurate steering. Introduce increased righting moments to build speed before bearing off to increase apparent angle change.

Top Tip
Always keep looking over your shoulder for gusts and try to stay in areas of strongest wind, you can then sail lower and faster.

Roll u'r Buddy (2 boats)

INTERMEDIATE **ADVANCED**

Gear – None.

Description – A paired exercise that's basically a downwind match race. The 2 boats start overlapped with the windward boat always trying to roll its partner. The leeward boat is always trying to protect its wind and move forward or gain depth whenever possible. Whenever the leeward boat gets rolled it will look to gybe off and get an opportunity to regain an advantage. The other boat then gybes and its aim is to pull off a slam-dunk when they next meet. When a boat passes clear ahead on the opposite gybe the exercise is restarted.

Aim
- Attacking and defending options downwind.
- Boat handling.

Set up – Start on a beam reach nose to tail and bear away onto a downwind course on the count of 3. Boats should try not to become separated or to luff too hard as this would be unrealistic in a championship situation. When one boat crosses clear ahead on an opposite tack, re-set and swap the lead boat.

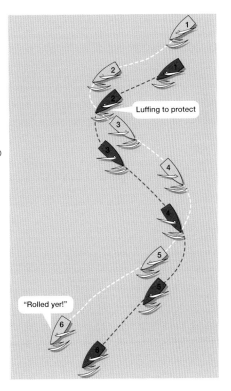

Coaching Points
- Advanced It's all about timing when you sail high for speed and low for depth.

Kill Zone (2+boats)

INTERMEDIATE **ADVANCED**

Gear – 3 marks.

Description – This is a biased course exercise with a downwind focus. The boats round the windward mark nose to tail on the starboard lay line, then have three overtaking opportunities: The bear away, the gybe or the leeward mark rounding. Depending on where you are you may be attacking or defending. The game is still to be first to the windward mark defending the left or right – depending on the course bias. If you choose the leeward mark on the non-favoured side you must tack as soon as possible to keep the drill realistic. Once boats reach the windward mark they wait for the last boat to restart the next lap as the leader.

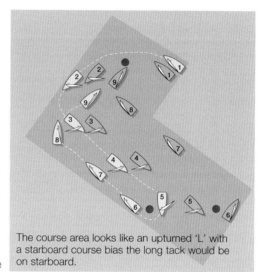

The course area looks like an upturned 'L' with a starboard course bias the long tack would be on starboard.

Aim
- Reinforce the importance of key overtaking areas.
- Rotate the fleet to mix up abilities at the front.
- Provide overtaking practice on a one sided course.

Set up – Lay a leeward gate and then drop a windward mark 100-200 metres upwind depending on ability and class of dinghy. This mark will need a 15° to 20° bias to the port or starboard depending on the side you want the course to be biased. Next get the fleet to line up on starboard tack just above the lay with about 10 seconds of sailing remaining before the mark.

Variations – Use alternate sides and amounts of course bias to vary the drill. Also try a port tack approach – best started with a 'rabbit' start.

Coaching Points
- Advanced Again place an emphasis on knowing when to go for speed and when to go for depth. Accurate lay lines and pressure awareness are key overtaking weapons.

Tactical Exercises

Most exercises can be used with a tactical focus, not just those specifically designed for the purpose. Once again, if scenarios are being introduced for the first time you should use a 'dinghy park shuffle', (see page 66).

Crews Call (2+boats)

Gear – 2-4 marks and a coach boat.

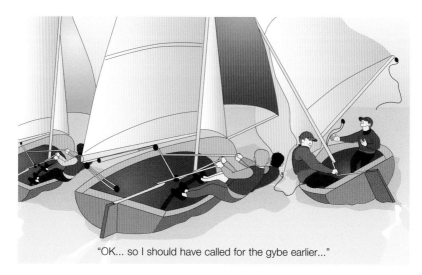

"OK... so I should have called for the gybe earlier..."

Description – Only the crew is allowed to talk during this exercise. That means all decisions have to come from the crew and the information can only be shared one way. The boats must race around a course of your choice and must adhere to all the racing rules.

Aim
- Improve the tactical awareness of the crew.
- Build the crew's self worth.
- Highlight the importance of communication and shared responsibility.

Set up – Lay a windward/leeward, triangle or trapezoid and use a 3, 1, GO, sequence.

Variations – After running this exercise a couple of times, swap the calls over to the helm and repeat.

Coaching Points
- Start After swapping around the roles debrief on how this impacted the decision making as a fleet. Then get the sailors to talk through the differences within their individual boats and what they can learn from the exercise.

Solo Piggy (2 or 4 boats)   START

Gear – 2 to 3 marks.

Description – A simple introduction to covering. One boat will be designated the 'piggy' and must try and escape the other boats' cover. The covering boat must keep themselves between the 'piggy' and the next mark or slow the 'piggy' by using a tight cover. Once a lap of the course has been completed the positions are reversed. If at any point the 'piggy' breaks cover they then become the covering boat.

Aim
- Introduce tight and loose covers.
- Reinforce dirty air theory.

Set up – Lay a course of your choice with set number of laps. Start a 3, 1, GO sequence.

Coaching Points
- Start At the briefing introduce the fundamentals of a tight cover and the lee bow effect. Get the sailors to put the theory into practice and comment on their effectiveness.

Piggy in the Middle (3 or 6 boats) INTERMEDIATE

Gear – 2 to 3 marks.

Description – The rules for the game are simple. The lead boat has to try and send the middle boat to the back of the fleet. He or she can do so by giving the 'piggy' a penalty, blocking out the 'piggy' on a bad shift or sailing him over a lay line or by giving them dirty air. As soon as the last placed boat changes, the fleet re-assigns roles to match the new order. The winner is the boat that finishes as the 'piggy', with the last placed boat being the loser.

Aim
- Teach boats covering techniques.
- Match race practice.
- Rules practice.

Set up – Lay a course of your choice with set number of laps. Start a 3, 1, GO sequence. As soon as the boats are underway the game starts with the coach acting as umpire and video boat.

Coaching Points
- Start At the briefing introduce the fundamentals of a tight cover and the lee bow effect. Get the sailors to put the theory into practice and comment on their effectiveness.
- Intermediate In the briefing generate ideas on how to break cover. If the fleet is not fluid then use the coach boat to create an opening or re-start.

Match Racer (even numbers)

INTERMEDIATE

Gear – 3 marks and coach boat.

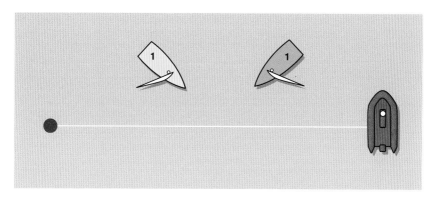

Description – Start by electing port and starboard ends and then use a 3, 2, 1, GO, sequence. On the 2 minute gun the boats will sail downwind through the line and start the match. From this point the aim is to use the racing rules and their boat handling skills to out-start the other boat and then beat them around 2 laps of a windward leeward course. Then repeat the match changing their starting ends.

Aim
- Improve racing rules knowledge.
- Improve boat handling and using tight cover.

Set up – Start by laying a windward/leeward course approximately 200-400 metres in length. Lay a start line below the leeward mark and begin the sequence. Once the race has started the coach takes on the role of umpire and will give tack or gybe penalties to those boats that infringe. Repeat the match for a best of 3 or 5 regatta. If running multiple starts, the matches must umpire themselves and if a penalty cannot be decided upon then both boats will be deemed to have infringed.

Variations – Try leaving all marks to starboard to change the approach situations.

Coaching Points
- Intermediate In the debrief talk through protecting the favoured side of the course and the difference between a loose and tight cover. Highlight any rule situations that occurred which need to be explained.

Dinghy Park Shuffle

This is a great method to coach the rules, tactics and general race course skills in a 3 dimensional way. It should always be used as a shorebased rehearsal prior to coaching rules tactics or any on the water exercises that requires judgement of time and distance.

The basic principle is simple. Tie your dinghies to their trolleys and push them around the car park or dinghy park to simulate scenarios around the race course.

The idea was developed for coaching team racing but we quickly found that it was excellent for coaching rules and tactics for beginners and experts alike.

Coaching Transits

Exercise A (without boats)

- Create a start line with old tyres or cones.
- Get each sailor to stand on one end and use an object in the distance as their transit marker.
- When they have finished get them all to stand downwind of the line, walk towards

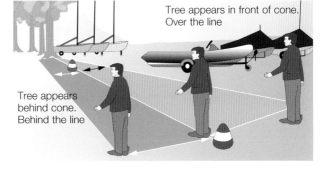

Tree appears in front of cone.
Over the line

Tree appears behind cone.
Behind the line

the line and stop when they think they are on the line, assessing how good their transit actually was.
- Get all the sailors to step 2 paces forward and tell you what has happened to their transit. It should now be forward of the start line buoy or the start boat. The rule is – if the transit is forward of the buoy then they are over the line.
- Get the sailors to then take 2 paces behind the line and repeat the process. The rule is – if the transit is behind the buoy then they are behind the line.

Exercise B (with boats)

This time the sailors need to tie their boat to their trolleys and push them from the transoms upwind towards the start line, stopping when they think their bow is on the line. Ideally they should approach on a close hauled course. Once they have positioned their boat they should then join the coach at the start boat to examine how close their boat is to the start line.

Repeat the process until they are confident about being on the line every time.

Coaching Tactics and Rules

Example rule: Coaching mark roundings (Rule 18)

Exercise A: 3 boat lengths!
- Using a mainsheet or length of line, measure 3.5 boat lengths.
- Place a buoy (tyre or cone) in the centre of the dinghy park and arrange the sailors in a circle, facing in, approx 10 boat lengths away from the buoy.
- Get all of the sailors to walk towards the buoy and stop where they think they would be when their boat enters the 3 boat lengths zone. Because they are sitting halfway down the boat the actual distance is 3.5 boat lengths.
- By tying the rope to the buoy you can scribe a 3.5 boat length circle and judge how good your sailors are at judging distances.

This exercise can be repeated with line measuring 4.5 boat lengths which would be the distance where you start asking for room prior to rounding the mark if you were overlapped.

Exercise B: Rule 18
Set up a top mark and get 2 sailors to push their boats from the transom.
Boat 1 should stop when they think the bows have just entered the 3 boat length zone.
Boat 2 should place theirs to leeward of boat 1 but with a slight overlap. This requires good judgement of distance and may require some 'tweaking' to get it right.
The coach can then start to ask the sailors the difference in responsibilities of each boat when rounding the mark either with or without an overlap. In each case the coach needs to refer to the definitions of **keep clear, mark room and proper course.**
Key rules that need to be read are
Rules 11 (windward/leeward).
Rule 18 (mark-room)
Rule 14 (avoiding contact).

Coaching Points
To focus on what each boat must do and try to link this to tactics. Another technique is to compare this rule with a car going around a roundabout, giving the other boat time and opportunity to get around safely and fairly.

Part 3 - General Training

Mixed Ability Exercises

All sailors learn differently and the coach needs to be able to create a learning environment that pushes everyone to want to learn. This section enables the coach to control who leads the race, it develops confidence, keeps the group together, pushes the better sailors and allows the less experienced ones to see how the top sailors do it.

Follow on Racing (4+boats) START INTERMEDIATE ADVANCED

Gear – 3 marks and a coach boat.

Description – Boats initially start together on the same sequence then after each lap the leading boats are held back to regroup the fleet. The race continues for a pre-determined number of laps.

"Green, you start next whistle"

Aim
- Give the less able sailors a chance to compete around the whole course.
- Keep the fleet together to encourage boat on boat situations to develop.
- Make the race more challenging for more proficient sailors.

Set up – Set a windward/leeward course approximately 200-300 metres in length with the start/finish line doubling as a mid-course gate. Start the race as usual and get boat to pass through the mid-course gate both upwind and downwind. If a gap has developed hold the leaders back at the gate to reform the fleet.

Variations – Sending the leader to the back of the fleet each time they pass the gate is another fun way of running mixed ability racing.

Coaching Points
- Start When sailing next to a sailor of higher ability use that time to compare your sail set-up, boat balance, trim and technique. They are obviously doing something better, so what is it?
- Advanced Sailing through the fleet can require you to depend more on your compass as the fleet may not be in sync with the shifts.

Split Starts (4+boats)

START

Gear – 4 marks and start boat.

Description – A simple way of starting a mixed ability group.
• Less able sailors start to windward of the advanced group so that they approach the windward mark at roughly the same time.
• Advanced sailors will have to fight through dirty air to get to the front of the fleet while others get clear air and the opportunity to lead the race.

Aim
• Put sailors in unfamiliar situations.
• Get productive racing out of a group with mixed ability.

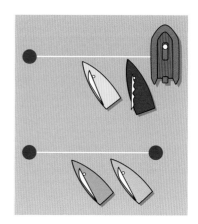

Variations – Pair the sailors up so that they are matched with another boat on the other line. The winning team will have the best combined score.

Coaching Points
• Start/Advanced Pair the sailors to coach each other. This way the start sailors get instruction from people who really know what they are doing and advanced sailors have to think about what makes them fast and reinforces their understanding.

Handicap Pursuit (4+boats) START INTERMEDIATE ADVANCED

Gear – 2-4 marks and coach boat.

Description – Using a course of your choice give sailors a ranking in order of ability with 1 being the lowest in ability. Using a rolling clock depending on the length of course, start sailors at 10 or 30 second intervals. Sailors will then sail a predetermined number of laps with the finishing order being the final positions of the race.

Aim
- Find equilibrium in the fleet with all sailors having to work equally hard to compete.
- Should finish with all the boats close together.

Variation – With smaller fleets the finishing order of each race when reversed will be the starting order of the next race. When there have been the same number of starts as there are boats, the finishing order of that race will be deemed the final results for the day and prizes awarded accordingly. If this system is used keep it secret so boats cannot attempt to sandbag for the final.

Boredom Beaters

Fun as a FUNdamental

Fun is the one aspect of sailing we can easily forget when rushing around the race course and yet it is the factor that keeps people in the sport, especially when young. The added benefits of games within this section are that it also teaches skills without the sailor noticing. Remember to smile and remind sailors they need to smile!

Top Tip
Work hard to keep clear air and plan ahead especially at round markings.

One Rule Racing (2+boats)   START

Gear – 2-4 marks and a coach boat.

Description – Using a standard race format, and the only rule is, no collisions (both boats are disqualified if this does occur). Excessive roll tacking, gybing and pumping is allowed. Best used on light wind days.

Aim
- Introduce and refine speed enhancing techniques.
- Fun and physical.

Set up – Standard course and sequence.

Coaching Points
- Start Video the boats that are better at enhancing speed and get them to comment on what they are doing.

Reverse the Race   START

An adaptation on standard racing is to simply reverse the race whenever the coach blows the whistle. This means that racing always remains close and the faster boats have to win back the places while the slower boats get to see what the faster boats are doing.

Grand Prix Starts (2+boats)   START

Description – This race starts with all boats on shore (they could even require rigging). Sailors line up and when the whistle/gun goes they race to their boat, rig and launch before racing around a course and finish by returning the boat to its original state on shore.

Aim
- A fun alternative to conventional racing.

Variation – This could use a relay format with each team handing over to another and so on.

Reversing Race (3+boats) START

Gear – 2 marks and coach boat.

Description – Starting between the coach boat and a mark, sailors must reverse downwind to the finishing mark. The first boat to complete the course wins.

Aim
- Improve reversing boat control.
- Challenge all abilities with an unfamiliar skill.
- Fun and out of the ordinary.

Set up – Lay a windward and leeward mark about 100 metres apart. Line all boats up in stationary position to windward of a line between the top mark and the leeward mark. Using a 10 second countdown start the boats and then follow them downwind to finish at the bottom mark.

Safety First – Always get the helm to push the tiller towards the boom when exiting sailing backwards.

Variations – It's possible to run this exercise as a windward/leeward team relay.

Coaching points
- Start The direction you point the rudder is the way the boat will steer.
- Intermediate When initiating the reverse, get the bow just through head to wind before pushing the boom out. This will stop the boat spinning back to the position you started in.
- Advanced In high performance boats the helm will control the boom and the crew will focus on keeping the boat absolutely flat!

Dogfight (2+boats)

INTERMEDIATE

Gear – 1 bottle on string for each boat, 4 marks (optional) and a coach boat.

Descriptions – The aim of the game is to hit a plastic bottle attached to the end of a string trailing from the opponent's boat while defending your own. Sailors will be given a time limit and a sailing area in which to compete. Points are awarded for hitting an opponent's bottle and subtracted when your own is hit.

Aim
- Fun competition.
- Boat handling.
- Spacial awareness.

Set up – Brief the teams on the battlefield (sailing area) and send the teams to all corners prior to the start. Four buoys or other geographical features may mark the battlefield. A time limit can also be set.

"Did you actually put a message in the bottle?"

New Balls Please (1+boats)   START

Gear – 8 coloured tennis balls, 4 marks and a coach boat.

Description – A fun boat control exercise
involving collecting as many balls as
possible within a set time. All boats must be
outside the box designated by the 4 marks.
On the start signal the boats enter the box
and start collecting. The next signal signifies
the end of the game. The boat that collects
the most balls is the winner.

"New balls please!"

Aim
- Controlling speed.
- Boat handling.
- Enjoyable competition.

Set up – Lay 4 marks to form a square with each side about 50 metres in length.
Get the boats outside the box and throw in the coloured balls (colour can designate
value). Give the boats a 1 minute whistle and start the fleet calling back any boats
inside the box at the whistle. After 2 minutes signal the end of the game and count
the balls and their value to determine the winner.

Captain Splash (2+boats)   START

Description – The aim of the game is to capsize on the whistle and perform a series
of set tasks and right the boat in the shortest time. The tasks may be a selection of
the following: Pull the centre-board down, uncleat mainsheet, kicker or jib sheet, drop
spinnaker, swim the bow through the wind, turtle and right the other way. The boat
must then be righted and sailing at speed before the exercise ends.

Aim
- Emphasise the importance of certain actions in making capsize recovery faster
  and less strenuous.
- Take some of the fear factor away from capsizes.

Set up – Get the fleet within a set area then blow the whistle. Blow a second whistle
to end the drill when the first boat is recovered and sailing at full speed.

**Safety First – Ensure the conditions and ability of the group are appropriate for
the drill. Generally run this exercise at the end of a session to avoid
hypothermia. Make sure you have sufficient safety cover and keep a check
on all the capsized boats and their crews.**

Self Training Exercises

Coaching the sailor to be their own coach. The coach should always strive to get sailors to train themselves. The majority of the exercises in this book can be modified to be run by a single sailor in a group. This section looks at some more exercises specifically aimed at helping the sailor to develop racing skills. Self training is essential for making boat handling smooth and controlled.

Shore Drills (1 boat)   START INTERMEDIATE **ADVANCED**

Gear – 1 boat, trolley tie down lines, secure tie down points, an inflatable mark and a video camera.

Description – The most effective way to teach new boat handling techniques or refine routines in the boat. Simply identify the technique you wish to work on and perform it on land as you would on the water. Using a video camera record some footage of the sailors performing the technique and comment on the footage. If possible, look at some best practice footage of the same manoeuvre and identify the similarities and difference. Work on refining the technique, introducing the improvement identified.

Aim
- Improve speed, consistency, poise and balance in the boat.
- Identify asymmetry.
- Provide a variable free environment to teach a new technique.

Set up – Start by placing the boat on a well fitting trolley and raising the bow so the boat is level. Place the inflatable mark (or tyres) under the transom to support the back of the boat and then tie the bow and the shroud point down to secure fixing points on the ground. For trapeze boats it is also a good idea to support the mast. This is straight forward on twin wire boats as you can simply use the other set of wires.

Coaching Points
The best way to teach complex skills is to break them down into smaller components. By teaching each part in detail you simplify the learning process. Repeat the part until it is consistent then add it back into the complete technique. Whole-Part-Whole.

The Standard Hour (1 boat) START INTERMEDIATE ADVANCED

Description – An agreed routine that boats will practise each time they go sailing on their own. It cuts time wasting and ensures what area needs to be worked on gets done before any other distractions creep in. In its simplest form it may look like this:
- 20 tacks.
- 20 gybes.
- 5 minutes on each tack with perfect trim while checking compass readings.
- 5 straight sets, 5 straight drops (port rounding).
- 5 gybe sets, 5 gybe drops.
- 2 penalty turns.
- 3 practice starts on starboard.
- 1 port approach start.
- Reverse, double tack and holding position.
- Gut Buster.

Aim
- Keep sailing focused and ensure the foundations of good boat handling are kept fully oiled!

Set up – Agree the time you are going to meet and the time you hit the water. Have the list of exercises memorised and not stop until all the boxes are ticked.

Variation – If a weakness is identified during a regatta, discuss how that technique can be practised and include it in the standard hour replacing another exercise that is either ineffective or no longer in focus.

Coaching Points
Debrief after every session. Analyse and identify refinements, then develop!

RYA Laser Handbook
RYA G53

By Paul Goodison

Fantastic book by Britain's top rated Laser sailor who raced at the Olympics in 2008. Not only all you need to know about sailing and racing a Laser, but also lots of useful tips and information for dinghy racers in general. Highly recommended.

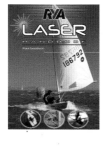

RYA Racing Rules of Sailing
RYA YR1/2009-2012

The complete Racing Rules of Sailing including RYA Prescriptions. This 186-page booklet is published in an easy-to-use, spiral bound, pocket size format.

RYA Crew to Win
RYA G39

By Joe Glanfield

Joe Glanfield progressed from crewing a Cadet at the age of 9 to winning a Silver Medal at the 2004 Olympics, crewing a 470 with Nick Rogers. This book is a mine of information on racing a trapeze boat with a symmetrical spinnaker, plus there's a small 49er section to keep skiff racers happy.

RYA Handy Guide to the Racing Rules
RYA YR 2009-2012

Most dinghy racers will never need to consult the complete Racing Rules. This little booklet summarises all you need to know to handle most situations, with easy-to-understand full colour illustrations to explain each major rule. What's more, it's printed on tough coated paper. Every racer should have a copy!

RYA Tactics
RYA G40

By Mark Rushall

You not only have to sail the boat perfectly, you also have to be a cunning mastermind. Mark Rushall unravels and explains all the complexities of tactical sailing. This impressive book is without doubt the definitive tactical bible and provides a huge amount of information with great illustrations.

RYA Youth & Junior Racing Guide

This 56-page booklet provides a complete guide to youth and junior racing administered by the RYA. Information includes Squad Programmes and Pathways, Case Studies of sailors, specifications of Junior and Youth Classes, Coaching and the Volvo RYA Champion Club Programme. **FREE!** email: amy.packard@rya.org.uk

RYA Catamaran Handbook
RYA G46

By Jeremy Evans

Fancy racing a catamaran? Jeremy Evans explains all you need to know about sailing on two hulls, with the accent firmly on racing Tigers, F18s, Hobie 16s and other high performance cats.

RYA Optimist Handbook
RYA G44

By Alan Williams

All you ever wanted to know about racing Optimists and a lot more! A superb book packed full of information for Oppie racers and their parents.